NARRATING AUDIOBOOKS

Everything You Need to Know to Get Started

By Brittany Ann Schank

I want to give a huge thank you to all of the people who have supported me and encouraged me to continue reaching for my dreams. To my number ones, my family. My husband and children inspire me every day to be the best I can and remind me what life is about. Everything I do is out of a desire to better our family. No matter what I am doing, I always have you in mind. Thank you for always being my reason to push hard, reach for the stars, and smile along the way.

To those who made this book happen, thank you. This includes a wide variety of friends, who constantly push me, help me see some of my faulty thinking, and cheer me on.

To Amanda Folstrom, that you for editing this book (we all know it was a mess when you originally got it) and putting it into a format that makes sense. Your inspiring words meant the world to me.

To all of the readers, thank you. I truly hope this is helpful in reaching your dreams. I'm proud of you for taking this step to further your knowledge, income, and passions.

TABLE OF CONTENTS

INTRODUCTION

Welcome! It's always nice to know a little bit about the author of the book you are about to read (and in this case, narrating it as well). I get it, I'm the same way. So, here's my story and how it pertains to this book.

My name is Brittany Schank. I am a wife to an entrepreneurial husband who owns his dream lawn and snow care business. I am a mommy to two beautiful babies, who literally have changed the way I live my life every single day. I am a currently enlisted in the Air National Guard, where I have grown, matured, and found pieces of myself I never would have found over the last 13 years. I am a mental health therapist, where I walk alongside people who are going through some of their toughest life moments and just need a hand to hold and someone to tell them it's going to be okay, while also using my education and skills to help reshape the way they see themselves, life, and their worth. I am a YouTuber, where I create videos twice a week about life's struggles, self-help, relationships, mental health, mommyhood, audiobook narration, and everything in between. Feel free to find me on YouTube by searching for my name. I have quite a bit of fun on there! Lastly, I am an audiobook narrator and I love narrating books about self-help, business, mental health, parenting, and every now and then, a good fiction read.

I'd love to give you some elaborate story about how narrating audiobooks was a lifelong dream and after years and years of imagining it, I finally took the leap and that everything, including auditioning, editing, and narrating, all came easily for me. If I did say all that, I'd be totally lying. The real story is pretty legit too though. Here we go:

So, one day I was listening to a podcast about therapists building their own private practice and the gentleman being interviewed mentioned that he had written a book. He said the book was available in paper format, but would also eventually be out in audiobook format once the narration was complete. There was some sort of joking around about whether the guy narrated it himself or not, and he joked back and said he hired it out. He then mentioned the website (which, continue reading or listening, I swear I will give this gem of information away later) and I immediately went to it. Once I got to the website, I literally thought to myself "Well, this can't be THAT hard". I created a profile and perused around for a couple of hours trying to figure everything out. I searched on YouTube for some videos on narrating audiobooks, and surprisingly didn't find a whole lot of information besides how to edit via some editing software. So, blindly, I continued making my profile and perusing around.

I immediately stopped on the tab that talked about pay. I began dreaming of what some extra income could mean for my family, for my business, and for my future. I read about passive income and residual income. I thought about an extra $400, $800, $1,000 per month and felt delighted, weightless and inspired. I kept digging and researching.

After a couple hours of getting used to the site, I found a book that I thought might be okay to narrate because, let's be honest, I didn't think I was good enough for an actual "good book". There was a button to audition. I picked up my iPhone and used the voice recorder to record my voice while I was sitting in my daughter's bedroom trying to be as quiet as possible while she napped. Yeah, I'm sure that audio sounded fabulous! I knew NOTHING about editing software, how to edit, any specifications that needed to be met, really, I knew just enough to read what was in front of me and click the submit button. I submitted that audition and low and behold what do you know: I didn't get selected. I continued to increase my skills and auditioned for books over that week (yes, still using my iPhone) and to my surprise, was selected for a book! Not just any regular book, but one I thought I would actually pick off of a bookshelf myself to read! I was so excited and so scared all at the same time. I didn't' even know what I was doing, but boy oh boy was I excited to try!

I started searching for any and all information I could find.

I learned that I needed a microphone and editing software. I did some quick research of both, ordered a microphone, installed a software and BOOOM I was on my way to narrating an audiobook. After hours upon hours of learning how awkward it is to speak into a microphone, recording, re-recording, making mistakes editing, re-making mistakes editing, laughing, crying, late nights, and early mornings, I had completed my first book. I was over the moon! I mean really guys, I was over the moon!

I submitted all of my audio to the writer, the writer sent me the kindest email about how much she loved it, and the book was complete! Well, I thought it was complete. Until a couple week later I received an email stating that my audiobook didn't meet specifications. Specifications? I had no idea about specifications!

Not only did my recording not meet specifications, it didn't meet a TON of specifications that I didn't even know existed. Not only did I not know they existed, I had absolutely no idea how to fix them. I was sick to my stomach, wanted to cry, and wanted to quit. I spent the entire day sulking around not knowing what to do. After being a bear to be around, my husband finally said to me, "Just delete your account and pretend none of this happened." That was a viable option, but for anyone who knows me, knows I wasn't going to take that as an answer. I literally said to him "I've never accepted failure, and I'm not about to today." So, back to the drawing board it was.

Again, after hours and hours, and more hours and hours of research I found a really great forum of people who walked me through the process of what I needed to do next. Since there were so many things wrong with my original audio, I didn't know where to start. One of the items listed in the email, stated there was something wrong with the amount of background noise I had and that it sounded like a loud constant noise, like a sound machine. Quite honestly guys, I had to giggle. There, in fact, was a sound machine on in the background! Whoops! Well, at least I knew how to fix that problem. While working with this team on all of the other problems, it was decided the best thing for me to do was to re-record my audio, this time, the right way. After sulking in my sorrows for a bit, I regained my excitement to actually complete my first audiobook, again. I incorporated all of the advice I got and re-recorded the book.

The second recording sounded better because I already had practiced these words and I was using a real microphone. I finished the audio, submitted it, and a couple weeks later got an email stating the audiobook had passed the check and was now for sale! I was on cloud nine. I couldn't believe I actually did it! I was hooked.

I have auditioned for more books, have received more offers to record, and have sold over 100 books. It's become like a manualized process for me that takes little to no extra thinking. Now I know what I'm doing and I don't have to recreate the same book twice just to get it right.

So, why am I writing this book? I want to help others navigate their way through the audiobook recording process and not have to make the same mistakes I did. I hope to make this process simpler for those who know they want to narrate audiobooks as well as inspire those who are on the fence to take the leap! I hope to give you tips and tricks to make your job easier, to help you build an extra income for your family, and to help you accomplish something you may have always dreamt or never thought you'd dream. I hope to help you get started in the right direction so you can dream bigger than you'd ever imagined.

CHAPTER ONE: WHO IS LOOKING FOR THIS SERVICE?

Audiobook sales are on fire! People are listening to audiobooks on their commute to work, while they are working out, fishing, getting ready for the day, in the shower, on car rides, on vacation, on their lunch break, and lying in bed getting ready to fall asleep. Audiobooks are everywhere! Audiobook sales are on the rise and we don't foresee this changing anytime soon. Think about this: when is the last time you picked up a paperback book versus when is the last time you listened to an audiobook? Like I said, audiobooks sales are on fire and it's not a wonder that there are so many places you can go to utilize your audiobook narration skills.

If you google "audiobook narration", one of the first items you will see pop up will likely have something to do with ACX. ACX, Amazon, iTunes and Audible are all interrelated. ACX is currently the powerhouse behind audiobooks and are the leader in the production and sales of audiobooks. As I am writing this book, there are almost 1,500 books sitting inside of ACX waiting for a narrator to record them, and that's just today. ACX is a goldmine for anyone who has the desire and ability to narrate an audiobook.

Now, I couldn't leave this chapter without mentioning some of the other areas in which you can use your narration skills. Fiverr has a significant number of listings to hire audiobook narrators not to mention individuals to do something called "voice overs" all the time. The best way for me to explain a voice over is by comparing it to many of the commercials we see. When we see images flashing through the screen and a voice is talking, but in fact there is no one on the screen that is actually talking, that is a voice over. People are constantly looking for individuals to do voice overs for advertising purposes for both big and small gigs.

Moving forward in this book, I am going to speak about the first scenario I provided, which is narrating audiobooks with ACX. Don't worry guys, I have not been hired by them to produce this book, nor am I being paid to say anything that I am saying by them. This just so happens to be from where most of my experience has come and I have found great success there. I mean, let's be honest. ACX is the face of audiobooks so it only makes sense.

CHAPTER TWO: CAN I ACTUALLY NARRATE AUDIOBOOKS?

Alright friends, so here is the tough part. Not everyone can narrate audiobooks. There are a couple of key dos and don'ts that I would like to go over. Of course, these are my opinion, and if you find success against my opinions, please let me know, because I love me some success stories.

1. DO you have a desire to narrate audiobooks? I'm guessing you wouldn't be reading or listening to this if you didn't. But for real, explore your reasons for wanting to narrate and really sit in them. Are you wanting to narrate because you need some extra income, want to feel successful, or because it's always been a dream of yours? Have at it! Do you want to narrate an audiobook because you think it's going to be effortless.....meh.

2. DO you enjoy reading books? Guys, this is one of my favorite parts about narrating audiobooks. I literally get to read books that I would normally read for enjoyment and get paid for them! Seriously, it's a win win and I can't imagine it gets any better than this. If you dread reading books, this gig might not be for

you.

3. DO you have a good voice? Now, now, I'm not saying a good singing voice, or a voice with a really cool British accent (although that is super neat). I am also not asking you if you are in love with your own voice. In fact, when I started narrating audiobooks, I had no idea if other people thought I had a decent voice, annoying voice, harsh voice, etc. It wasn't until I got my first gig that I was affirmed that at least someone thought I had a halfway decent voice. Overall, do think you have a good voice? Are you able to speak clearly and are not often asked to repeat what you're saying? Can you slow down your speech when you're nervous or speed it up if you typically speak slowly? Do you make odd noises with your voice? Let me tell you friends, this is hard to know until you start recording yourself. Are you monotone or can you fluctuate the tone and pitch of your voice? Some people assume narrating audiobooks is done in the same manner you would read them: not true. Well, it could possibly be true if you're picturing the way an elementary school teacher would read a book to students (full of life, energy, and with an appropriate tone based on the book), but likely this is not how we read to ourselves in our head. Audiobooks need to be engaging. People legit return audiobooks based on the narrator's performance, so it can't be bland and lacking emotion.

4. DO you have technical abilities? Not like knowing how to create computer programs, but the ability to use a computer and learn new skills. There are a variety of audio recording software programs/packages available for you to use, but if you've never used audio recording software before, it can be somewhat complex or tricky to learn. I legitimately learned a majority of what I learned through YouTube video. If

you have already played around with audio recording software, you will be golden in this arena. If you find yourself struggle with simple techy things, audiobook narration might be a bit trickier for you.

5. DO you have extra time? The beauty in audiobook narration, is you work as much or as little as you want. This isn't like your normal 9:00-5:00 job where you are told to be there on certain days or hours of the week. On the flip side, you should be self-driven. If you need someone to tell you what to do and when, you do better with strict guidance, or you struggle to meet deadlines on your own, then audiobook narration may not be for you.

CHAPTER THREE: EQUIPMENT TO GET STARTED

With any new business adventure, the first question usually starts by inquiring about the startup costs. People want to see a quick return on their investment, and of course, the higher the startup costs, the longer it takes to get that return on your investment.

The interesting thing about most businesses is there is such a wide range of what people want versus need to get started in a business. Let's take a mental health therapist for example). To startup, a mental health therapist could rent a small space, find some gently used furniture, get a subscription to an electronic record system, create their paperwork, and begin seeing clients. That's a fairly simple way to get started. On the other hand, another mental health therapist could rent an office space with multiple offices so they can expand, get a subscription to a fancy, name brand electronic record system, pay to have their paperwork created, pay for their website to get created, hire an interior designer, order new furnishings for all offices, hire an administrative assistant, hire a social media expert, buy a new computer, and new wardrobe to fit their endeavor. Both are fine, I mean, who am I to judge. One takes on far more risk than the other. So, of course, the latter of the two startup scenarios probably will have nicer furniture, the space may feel more welcoming, the process might be somewhat smoother to maneuver and their furniture may last longer, but the first scenario describes someone who has much less overhead and much less work cut out for them just to break even, while still providing the same service the customer is looking for.

So, here's the good news for all of you. I literally started and completed my first 10 audiobooks with an investment of $44.99. What?! I know, it's crazy right. The $44.99 I spent was on a microphone. That one was a quick return on investment! This may or may not be the case for you because it just so happened the remainder of the equipment, I needed I already owned.

Here's a comprehensive list of what you need to get started in the audiobook narration business. I also feel like I need to add this equipment still is all I continue to use to get the job done.

1. A microphone. I purchased a microphone from Amazon. After reading through a significant number of reviews and talking to other audiobook narrators, it was very clear that I didn't have to spend an arm and a leg to get a good microphone. Like I said before, mine was under $50 and I continue to use this microphone today. My microphone plugs right into the USB port on my computer so it is super simple to use. I didn't have to install any programs to use it. It is literally plug and go.

2. A computer. You are going to need a computer to record, edit, audition, etc. I don't have an extremely high-quality computer and there is no need to get one for this purpose. It doesn't matter if you have a desktop or laptop or it runs Windows or Mac. Any of these will work just fine. It's truly about your preferences.

3. Computer Storage. The number of files you will be saving would take up a ton of space on your computer. It is important to have some sort of storage where you can save your files. This could be something as simple as a

thumb drive or external hard drive. You, as the narrator, will possess the only working copies of your audiobook. You will need to revert back to these files to make updates or changes and believe me when I say, it totally sucks to have to go back and re-record something because you didn't save it.

4. Audio Recording Software: This is what you will use to record your audio onto. You then make corrections to it by editing the saved recording. There's a wide variety of audio recording software out there. There are many that free and many you can pay hundreds of dollars to own. Some of the most commonly used software packages are Reaper, Audacity, Ocenaudio, Cool Edit Pro, and Twisted Wave. Each of them has their own advantages and disadvantages. It is extremely important to find the software that fits you best as this is where you will spend most of your time. It is estimated that for every hour of audio you produce, you can anticipate up to five hours of editing time. In my experience, this number was significantly reduced once I got familiar with and comfortable using the software I purchased. The first couple books I narrated may have even taken me longer than 5 hours of editing time per audio hour. Most software nowadays has fairly decent question and answer sections and, at the very least, we know YouTube will likely have tutorials. Make sure that you take some time to explore the different software packages, read their reviews, and talk to other narrators.

5. Quiet Working Space: So, embarrassing story alert. But for those of you who read or have listened to my introduction, remember that the first audiobook I created didn't pass the ACX inspection. Do you remember why? A sound machine guys, a sound machine! I record my audiobooks at night when my kids were asleep and we have sound machines in each of their rooms right next to where I record. Naturally, the sound machine noise

carried into my recording space. When I received the email from ACX stating my audio didn't meet specifications, it literally said it sounded like there was a sound machine in the background. Yep, there was, whoops! So again, this is something some people spend a ton of money on, but I truly don't believe that's necessary. I mean, I know it's not necessary. I haven't spent a ton of money on the room I do my audio in, but there are a lot of things to be cognizant of. If you start researching recording spaces you will see things like closed off rooms with sound eliminating material. Some people spend hundreds of thousands of dollars creating their space. That probably would be really nice and comfy to be in, but it's probably not in the budget for a new audiobook narrator who isn't sure if this is their type of gig or not. So what type of space do I recommend? A closet is an ideal space. The clothing absorbs most of the echoes and it's usually fairly quiet in a closet. If your closet is too small or just not an option for you, there are other places that will work, too. Small spaces are best because larger spaces have a lot of echo and air to their sound. Also, places with carpet are best as opposed to hard floors for the same reason. Rooms that don't have any furnishings also tend to echo a lot. So, wrapping this up, a small, carpeted, furnished space that is quiet (and doesn't have a sound machine playing) is best. The better your environment for recording, the less editing you will have to do to your audio.

6. Headphones: When I started editing, I thought my speakers would do just fine, but I quickly learned it just wasn't true. Most computer speakers can't pick up some of the really important sounds we listen for like breath sounds, mouth clicking, and swallowing sounds. At first, I was like, "Well, if I can't hear it neither will the person listening to the audiobook." Not true! A lot of people listen to audiobooks in the car where the vol-

ume is turned up way louder than someone listening on their computer or laptop. It is important to be able to hear these sounds so they can be edited out. Consumers return audiobooks to the narrators all the time due to noises just like these. Seriously friends, just get yourself some headphones.

CHAPTER FOUR:
FINDING YOUR NICHE

One of the most important and rewarding things I have found while narrating audiobooks is to make sure I choose books in a genre that I actually like. Yes, guys, you can narrate books that you would normally be interested in reading, so essentially, you get paid to read books that you would normally read. Okay, okay, of course there is more work that goes into it than this, but really, it's a win win situation!

Before you even beginning to look for books that are available to narrate, think about what type of books you like to read. Are you into fiction, non-fiction, self-help, romance, adventure, memoirs, travel, religion, or poetry? Do any of those make you want to jump up and down for joy to read or do any of those make you want to fall asleep? Do you remember back in school when you were forced to read textbooks in the subjects or genres you despised? How easy would it have been for you to have read those books aloud in an excited tone and to give them the time and energy they deserved? Would people have been able to hear in your voice that you were bored or uninterested in the subject? It's the same with audiobooks. It's hard to fake being interested in a book that you're narrating.

In addition to thinking about what types of books you want to narrate, begin thinking about books you are going to actively choose not to narrate. There are a whole host of books available that some people are comfortable narrating, while others might run from them due to content, subject matter, or even the emotions they may evoke from you. Some examples include books about sexual assault, erotica, or religion. There are books that involve active drug use, relationships with same sex partners, domestic violence, child abuse or abortions. Really rack your brain for some of the topics that you are not willing to narrate. It is important to know your limitations and set your boundaries beforehand.

I will never forget one of the first audiobooks I narrated which sounded like a great book. I read the summary of the book and submitted my audition. I was so honored and excited when I was selected to narrate the book! About halfway through the book, there was a gruesome sexual assault. I was not expecting that. It entirely threw me off guard and made me question if this was the type of narrating, I wanted to do. I had to ask myself about my morals and values and whether reading this book was how I wanted to represent my narrating abilities. I did some deep soul searching and decided it was something I was, in fact, okay with. But regardless, it took my breath away because I wasn't expecting it and hadn't considered yet if this was something, I was okay with or not okay with narrating.

Another niche to consider is whether you want to do books with multiple characters. There are a variety of fiction books that call for multiple voices. For example, think of Harry Potter. There are a multitude of characters with different personalities, voices, and temperaments. The more characters, the trickier it is to keep track of which voice is for who. These books are oftentimes more intricate in narration, but some narrators truly love this and seek out these types of books as offer a space for the narrator to get creative in their work and are fun to listen to.

I have heard of many different tricks narrators use to remember which character goes to which voice. For example, some narrators save a quick sample on their desktop with the character's name so at any point while they are narrating, they can go back and get a sample of what they chose that character to sounds like. Additionally, I have heard of narrators drawing out each character on paper, a whiteboard, or anything else that is easily accessible. You can draw the characters out in a family tree sort of style and write below them the things you want to remember about them and their voice. Also, some characters may require an accent, a stutter, or some other voice modifications. This is a nice way to quickly refresh your memory of the small, but unique details you created for them.

Self-help, biographies, dieting, and business books likely will only have one person's voice in them. Often times, these are informative books so your voice needs to be engaging. There isn't a lot of acting in these types of books, which make them great ones to start off your narrating journey to allow you to get comfortable with reading, hearing your voice, editing, and submitting your books. Some narrators prefer this style of book while others venture off to the trickier books to narrate. The choice is yours.

CHAPTER FIVE: EXPLORING ACX

As I stated before, ACX is the powerhouse and the face of audiobooks. I don't know of another audiobook company that compares to ACX. In fact, I truly don't think they have any competition in this business. When a book is produced on ACX, it is then sold on Audible, Amazon and iTunes- three of the major powerhouses for audiobook sales.

This book is all about saving you guys time so you can start narrating faster to make some cash so I want to explain a few things about ACX to help get your mind wrapped around how it all works. It's taken me a lot of time and experimenting with ACX to gain this insight and information. I feel like I need to add here again, I am not compensated by ACX for this book and they have not sponsored this in any way. Additionally, this information is straight from me, Brittany Schank, and this is not the view of ACX.

First things first, when you log onto ACX, the first thing you need to do is create a profile. During this initial process they will ask for your personal information including your banking information and tax ID so they can send your earnings straight to your bank account and W-2 at the end of the year for tax collection purposes. You won't get any checks in the mail from ACX, it is all direct deposit. Both of these need to be completed before you can start narrating audiobooks for them so be sure to do all this first.

Once you've provided your financial information so they can pay you, you move on to create the rest of your profile. You'll select genres in which you are interested, what type of renumeration you prefer (check out the next chapter for more info on this), the length of the audiobook, your gender, unique voice qualities (accent, language, etc.), and a variety of other identifying factors. Audiobook writers can view your profile at any time.

Once your profile is complete, you are ready to start auditioning for audiobooks. Writers can search for you or you can audition for specific audiobooks. Let me be honest with you guys though, I have only once - let me repeat only once - been pursued by a writer to narrate their audiobook and, continuing on the honesty streak, the pay they were offering was too low even to consider. I selected and auditioned for every book I narrated. Here is a golden nugget of advice: when you are searching for a book for which to audition, look for the drop-down box on the top of the screen to allow you to sort the books by the date they were posted to ACX. This will allow you to see the most recent books uploaded to ACX first or by Amazon Sales-Bestselling (i.e., the books that have sold the best on Amazon appear the highest on the list). I almost always sort by bestselling so I know the books for which I am auditioning are sellers. When I started narrating audiobooks those dropdowns did not exist so this is a big-time saver. In fact, I narrated several books that didn't sell and one book I narrated that to this day hasn't sold a single copy. That's kind of crazy right guys? Like not even our moms or grandmas wanted to buy this book it was that bad! Truly, that piece of advice will save you time and money!

Once you have found an audiobook that meets your criteria, you can audition. Please ya'll, don't do what I did and audition with your iPhone. I'm giving you the tools and tips to audition the right way. Each book has an audition script from which you are expected to read. Use all the skills I have taught you so far, give yourself a pep talk, pat yourself on the back, and remind yourself that you're a Rockstar - audition for your first book!

The first time you read the script it might sound terrible.

That's okay. Delete and repeat. Don't be too hard on yourself. Give yourself another pep talk and another pat on the back. Don't forget to tell yourself you're a Rockstar. Now click the submit button. That's its friends, you just auditioned for your first book narrator role. Hooraaaah!

CHAPTER SIX: HOW MUCH MONEY WILL YOU MAKE?

If there was one question that I get asked just about every single time I talk to people about narrating audiobooks, this would be the one. Of course, this is extremely important because I can't imagine we would have many narrators out there if there wasn't pay associated with it. And of course, there should be pay associated with it. It's a talent and a skill! So, here's the nitty gritty on payment for audiobook narration.

There are two types of pay you can accept for audiobooks: per finished hour (PFH) and Royalty Share Deal. There are pros and cons to both, times and places to use both, and some cautions I need to share with you regarding them.

Let's start with per finished hour (PFH). A per finished hour payment is based upon the length of the book. The amount paid to a narrator for PFH work can vary anywhere from $0 to $1,000 per hour. That can sound like great money especially when you are talking $200, $300, $400, or $800 per hour! But guys, caution! This is not the amount of time it takes you to record and edit the book. This is the actual amount of time the book is once you have fully completed narrating it.

So, remember back to the beginning when we were talking

about one hour of recording equals up to five hours of editing time? This is where that tidbit of information is oh so important. Translated that means if you accept a PFH deal that pays $50 per hour (which MANY of them do), you are likely accepting your gig for $8 or less per hour. That's not even minimum wage in the state I live in not to mention narrating audiobooks is a skill that not everyone can do. You need to be compensated appropriately for your hard work, skill and knowledge.

On the flip side, at just about any given time, I see books on ACX that have a PFH rate of $200 or more. This can be much more lucrative and worth your time. The beauty in the PFH rate is you are guaranteed to get paid so long as you finish the project and you know exactly what your pay is going to be.

I also like to point out that for those of us who accept the $50 PFH rate, you are downplaying the worth of our skills. When writers are able to get people to narrate their audiobooks for that small of an amount of money, they keep come to expect it. Increase your worth my friends! You'd be doing us all a favor.

Moving on to the Royalty Share Deal. This, right here, is the main reason I chose to start narrating audiobooks. I was looking for ways to create a passive income. This pay option is what made narrating audiobooks an amazing opportunity for me. A Royalty Share Deal is where the publisher and narrator split the profits from the audiobook. For example, if the profits from a book are $8.00 per book, the publisher would get $4.00 per book sold and you, the narrator, would get $4.00 per book sold. Of course, ACX takes their share of the book first then after that the profits are split evenly! Of course, the downfall to this, is if you select a book that doesn't sell well, you're return on investment will be extremely low. If no books sell at all, you will receive $0.

However, if you narrate a book that sells well, the income can keep coming and coming. There is no cap to how much or how little you can make. This is where passive income is at its finest. You may put 20 hours into narrating an audiobook that makes you money for years and years to come! Of course, the downfall to this, is if you select a book that doesn't sell well, you're return on investment will be extremely low. If no books sell at all, you will receive $0.

There are tons and tons of success stories out there of people who continue to make $5,000, $10,000 $15,000 a month from royalty share deal narrations. The goal is to ensure you are picking books to narrate that are likely to sell (and using that handy dandy filter that sorts books available for audition by what's on the bestseller list).

Of course, there is a downside to Royalty Share Deals. I'm sure you've picked up on it, but you never know if a book is going to sell or not. Remember my story earlier about the book that still hasn't sold a single copy? That's the risk you take. I like to call it "donating my time". I'm kidding guys. It's a loss.

With all that said, you have two ways in which to be paid for narrating audiobooks. Both are viable options, but if I were in a position where I needed money quickly, I would start auditioning for per finished hour books. If I was looking for more of a residual income that I would make over time, I would choose the royalty share deal. Also, the book helps me decide which one to choose as well. If there is a book, I am interested in that is paying $400 -$600 per finished hour and it looks like a book that likely won't sell well, PFH is likely a wiser deal to take. Vice versa, if there is a book that appears to be extremely popular and the rights holder is offering $50 per finished hour (the royalty share deal option), I give it a quick "buh bye". Remember guys, there are tons of new narration opportunities as books are uploaded daily!

CHAPTER SEVEN: ACCEPTING A GIG

So, you gave yourself a pep talk, patted yourself on the back, reminded yourself that you're a Rockstar, and auditioned for your first book narration role. You may have received a couple emails saying: "Thanks for auditioning, but you were not selected to narrate this book". If so, it's okay! Congrats on following through with auditioning and gaining the experience! Don't be too hard on yourself and keep chugging along!

One of the best lessons I have learned from this process is when I am not selected for a book it's usually not because my voice is terrible, my editing skills stink, or that I can't read. It's usually because my voice just wasn't what the rights holder had pictured for that specific book. There was one time I was declined so many times in a row that I submitted my audio to a Facebook group of narrators and asked them to critique me. I got the same feedback I shared with you. There was nothing wrong with my voice or editing. I just likely wasn't the right fit.

I also think it's important to know that most people audition many times before getting an offer. As of today, I have a 29.2% audition to offer rate meaning I audition almost four times before being offered a gig and that's after doing it for some time. Give yourself some grace and keep trying.

Now, let's talk about when you actually receive your first

offer! Whoop whoop! Seriously, pat yourself on the back, jump up and down, whatever you need to do in order to feel the sense of accomplishment and pride you deserve! You're amazing and on the road to a fabulous narration journey! Congratulations!

Now, before pushing the accept button, tap the brakes right quick! Likely you received a message stating you received an offer. Please, please (did I say please), read through the offer in its entirety. Some of the big points to hone in on are the pay and timeline. Make sure the pay is what you expected. Sometimes, books are listed at PFH/royalty share. Make sure they are offering you the one you wanted. If it's PFH, make sure it is at the rate you are requiring. You have the ability to email the rights holder at this point to clarify or request a higher rate. They may not give you a higher rate, but if it's under what you require, give it a shot. It can't hurt anything. The rights holder cannot move on to offer another person the gig until you have declined it by pressing the decline button.

Once you have ensured the pay is correct, check out the timeline to complete the book. There are two deadlines listed. One is when the first fifteen minutes is due and the second is when the entire book is due. Remember to calculate out the time it will take you to complete this book based upon the one hour of audio equals five hours of editing. Really think that out as to whether that is a realistic timeline for you or not. Think ahead to holidays, work scheduled, etc. to ensure they are deadlines you can meet.

Okay, story time. Remember back to that offer I told you I received where the rights holder sent me an offer without me auditioning for the book, which is the only book this has ever happened to me on? Not only did they offer me an extremely low rate, they wanted the first fifteen minutes completed in 24 hours and the entire book completed in 48 hours. I mean, it was only a one-hour long book, but seriously, that's ludicrous.

Once you have completely reviewed the offer including pay and deadlines, it is time to decide what you are going to do. If this fits for you, go ahead and accept, but if it doesn't feel right, then decline. Remember, narration opportunities for books are uploaded daily! There's no need to accept something that doesn't jive with you.

CHAPTER EIGHT: COMPLETING YOUR AUDIOBOOK

Congratulations! You've accepted your first gig! I'm guessing if you're anything like me, once you clicked that button, your heart skipped a beat, you broke out in a small sweat, and thought "What did I just do?" It's all right, you're normal!

The first thing I do once I accept a gig is to request the manuscript from the rights holder. The manuscript is a paper copy of the entire book. This is what you will read in order to complete the audio recording. The manuscript needs to be read word for word. Many of these books are copyrighted so it is important not to change anything on the manuscript without talking to the rights holder. This can be challenging because sometimes things are clearly incorrect such as sentence structure. Always email the rights holder to inform them and ask if they would like you to change it when you record it.

Next, while I am waiting for the manuscript, I start making timelines based on the deadlines I was given from the rights holder. For example, if I have a six-hour audiobook due in 60 days, I will pick times and dates to set aside for the recording process then set myself a deadline to have an entire completed recording.

From there I can set aside times and dates to complete the editing process with a final editing completion date. My goal always is to get the finished audiobook to the rights holder earlier than the date they requested. I have a 100% success rate of doing this. It helps me to breathe more easily when I have completed the project early.

I begin recording when I have my own dates and deadlines and I have the manuscript. Some people like to read through the entire manuscript before recording so they are familiar with book's plot, characters, etc. I chose not to. This is somewhat just my character, but I like to be surprised. I also like that my true reactions and emotions to the content of the book are raw in my recordings. If I don't know what's coming, I'm legitimately surprised and can then surprise the listeners. You can hear it in my voice when I record. Other people don't like that so much. I don't think there's a right or wrong answer. Do what makes sense to you. I record all of my audio before moving on to editing.

Here's a tip to keep in your back pocket. Seriously, pay attention here, it will save you in the long run. When you record your audio, you must keep your files organized.

I create a folder named after the title of the book. Inside that folder, I create three more folders titled "Unedited", "Edited", and "Final". Seriously guys, this is important. I promise you will come back to this later.

When I am recording my audio, I stop at the end of every chapter and save it by its chapter name in the "Unedited" folder. When I am ready to edit, I make a copy of it and place the copy, by chapter name, in the "Edited" folder. Once I have completed the audio and exported it into an MP3 format, I save that one in the "Final" folder, by its chapter name. The file you will upload to ACX is the MP3 file. Be sure to keep the other two files in case you need to make edits later on. Always, always, always save these three copies.

ACX has some specific requirements when submitting your audio recordings. The requirements may seem overwhelming, but I promise I'll help you get there. Here are a couple of the big ones:

- All chapters must have "room tone" which is a blank recording without saying anything. It must be 0.5-1 second at the beginning and 1-5 seconds at the end of the recording. This is super easy to get, just don't talk.
- You can only have one chapter per file.
- The RMS level must be between -23 dB RMS and -18dB RMS with a peak value of no higher than -3dB RMS and noise floor no higher than -60dB RMS. (Does that sound like gibberish? Yeah, it did for me too. Just wait for the next chapter when I give you the magical formula that will make this so easy to do.)
- Finally (and I saved the best for last), all narration must be submitted by a human. Seriously, I had to clarify that.

Friends, there are other requirements, but these were the biggies for me. Make sure you check out the requirements for yourself to make sure you are meeting them.

CHAPTER NINE: THE SECRET FORMULA TO EDITING

What you are going to see next took hours upon hours to get to. Remember my story about submitting my first full recording and receiving an email with a never-ending list of everything I did wrong including having a sound machine on? Well, in this never-ending list there were a bunch of notes about my RMS level, noise floor, and peak value being off. I literally had no idea what most of those meant and searched YouTube, Google, Facebook, and other online forums for answers as to fix it. I wanted a simple process that I could use over and over again and not have to understand all of the nitty gritty details in order to get my audio perfect and ready to pass all of the inspections required.

You see, once you have completed and submitted your audiobook, it goes through inspections to ensure it meets all of the criteria required. Lucky for you guys, I compiled my many hours of research and into a formula that you guys can use for every audio clip and get success 100% of the time. For those of you listening via audiobook, you're going to want a pen and paper here. Otherwise, just pop back to this spot of the book once you're ready to edit. Here we go:

1. The most important thing you can do is ensure you start off in a quiet space. None of this editing and formatting will work if you're not in a quiet space. For real ya'all,

get in a quiet space.

2. If you make a mistake while recording, instead of stopping your recording, removing the mistake, and then starting up again, just snap your fingers. This creates a very noticeable spike in your audio. Start recording again by repeating whatever sentence had the mistake in it. When you go back to edit, look for the spikes and know you can delete the content prior to the spike because the correct audio is after the spike. I always listen to the audio though to make sure I am deleting the right stuff. This will make your editing process so much faster! I wish I had learned this from the beginning!

3. Remember to ensure you have "room tone" at the beginning and ends of your audio and remove all of your errors before moving on to the effects in the next bullet. Your audio should be in perfect condition meaning no errors left, no spikes in your audio from snapping, and no excessive periods where there is no talking.

4. Alright, are you guys ready for the secret formula? This formula has given me a 100% success rate for Audacity. It has not been tested in other programs, but feel free to use it. If you do not have some of these options under your effects tab in your software program, you may have to Google and download the plugin. Do the following:

    a. Select an area where there is no talking, then click effect, noise reduction, get noise profile. Then, select all of your audio, click effect, noise reduction, Noise Reduction (dB): 6, Sensitivity: 6.00, Frequency smoothing (bands): 6, Noise: Reduce.

    b. Under effect, select equalization, select curve: low roll off for speech, length of filter: about 5000, OK.

    c. Under effect, select RMS normalize, target RMS level -20dB, OK.

    d. Under effect, select limiter, type: soft limit, input gain (left): 0, input gain (right): 0, limit to (dB) -3.5dB, Hold: 10, Apply Make-up Gain: No, OK.

5. There is a plugin called ACX check, that you can down-

load as well. If you google this plugin, you will find it. I select all of my audio and run this plugin prior to submitting any of my audio to ACX. It literally tells you if your audio will pass the ACX inspection or not.

6. Once I have run the ACX check and it has passed the screening, I save the file as an MP3 and upload it into ACX.

This secret formula has been a lifesaver for me. At some point, Audacity likely will be updated, changed, etc. and this formula will need to be updated/changed, but for the time being it's a sure-fire success!

CHAPTER TEN: TOP LESSONS LEARNED

Friends, some of this is going to be a recap, but since my mistakes were so time consuming and research so thorough, I want to reiterate my biggest tips for you!

1. Dream and dream big. Audiobooks can provide both quick emergency income and long-term passive income. Set your goals and go for it!

2. Do not ever accept an audiobook gig that goes against your morals and values. It is NEVER too late to turn back. I accepted an audiobook that appeared to be a great book when I read the summary and auditioned, but once I got the book the sentence structure made no sense. I literally felt guilty producing this book and expecting people to pay for it… the first chapter was great and the rest of the book was horrendous and made no sense. I emailed the rights holder and told them I couldn't move forward unless the content was fixed. I felt like a phony and that didn't feel ethical to me.

3. Set your standards and don't allow anyone to make you go below them. If you set a boundary that you will not accept jobs that pay less than $400 per finished hour, do not go below that. You are worth that

standard! If you decide you are only doing royalty shares, don't let someone talk you into the PFH rate. Hold strong!

4. Collaborate when in need! For real, when I wasn't sure how to edit properly, I was in dire need. I legitimately got so desperate I offered to pay someone to recreate the audiobook I had promised to do. I knew I made a commitment and I didn't want to leave the rights holder high and dry. Luckily, I had found some really awesome techy people that knew a lot about editing and helped me through it. The techies told me I was out of my mind wanting to pay someone to do my editing. They encouraged me to keep going and I am so glad I did! Find your crew! Reach out!

5. Narrate books you love and you will shine! I have narrated books I didn't love. I thought I needed to narrate whatever came to me to build my skills. I was partially right. I needed to build my skills, but my true passion was not in those books and it was clear in the final product.

6. Remember your name is tied to your work. This was one of the scariest parts of narrating for me. What if I forgot to edit something out of the audio? What if I stunk at acting? What if I narrated a book that was taboo? Everyone would know it was me! It's also something you can be proud of! Take a deep breath, recognize how amazing you are, and remind yourself that regardless of how perfect you try to be, we all make mistakes. Also, everyone else's opinion shouldn't matter so much!

7. Have fun! ACX requires your books to stay on their site for a minimum of seven years. If you are narrating for another site, agency, or person, clarify this. Regardless, your loved ones, your friends, your family, and the community get to enjoy your books for years and years to come. How cool for your siblings,

friends, kids, and parents to pull up and listen to an audiobook that you read!